Meeting Halfway

Poems of faith, love, and friendship

Mary-margaret Belota

* * * * *

Formatting by Debora Lewis arenapublishing.org

ISBN-13: 978-1539539629
ISBN-10: 1539539628

Contents

FORWARD

These poems explore various aspects of the three foundational pillars of my life: faith, love, and friendship. Through no fault of my own, I have been enormously blessed with generous portions of each, and therefore would like to dedicate this volume to the two people who so lovingly provided that foundation for me: my parents,

Iris Tunnell Burns

and

E. B. Burns, Jr.

Though they have both gone on to glory, I think of them—with joy—every day, and thereby carry them with me always.

I would also like to extend special thanks to Mike Baldwin, poet extraordinaire, and long-time friend, without whose help and encouragement this volume of poems would not have come to fruition.

THE ETERNAL SPRING

From the bleakest landscape of this world
a determined blossom will spring.
In the echoless silence of this world
a bird will open its throat and sing.

In the insular indifference of this world
a smile will greet a lonely face.
From the deepest sorrow of this world
grief will be borne in an embrace.

From the fathomless darkness of this world
will rise the hues of early morn.
On the final, crowning day of this world,
somewhere a baby will be born,
and there will yet be hope.

EVANESCENCE

Adrift –
you say you feel adrift.
I feel I've been set free.
It seems we've changed positions yet again.
Once I cultivated the still waters
to anchor your racing heart.
Now you seek the tranquil cove
to keep me from the rapids.

Where lies the wiser course?
Does enlightenment incite the whitecap
to spend itself in froth at land's end?
Or does sapience dwell
in the gentle swell whose lull
belies its power?

We are merely motion,
vaporous tracings on faces in flow,
clinging,
floating,
moored in longing,
and buoyed
on tides of love.

MEETING HALFWAY

This is a poem to my friend, Kathe,
for whom the qualifying term "best"
is – at best –
inadequate.
How do you describe
a connection of the heart,
recognized instantly
    on some subterranean level,
and sustained
    through adolescent dreams and traumas,
until it becomes a conscious treasure
more precious than sunlight?
How do you measure the value
of meeting halfway,
whether between houses
or viewpoints?
What price can be placed
on absolute acceptance
at a time when variations from the norm
were unacceptable
and few things were absolute?
That we are so much alike
is perhaps less significant
than that we are different.

For through countless hours
of silliness and laughter,
    you of the silent, shaking variety,
    I from the school of screamers,
of entrusted confidences
of whispered hopes and aspirations,
you have shown me the world through a different eye,
an artist's eye,
an adventurer's eye –
and my vision has been enriched.
That small mound of earth is long since leveled
and the vacant lot was built on years ago,
but I see in that halfway point,
    born of shared fears and support,
the essence of our bond.
So I write this for you, Kathe,
    from the halfway point of our lives
for all the times you
recognized,
accepted,
shared,
trusted,
laughed,
listened,
and met me more than halfway.

CONTROL

Daily I am struggling onward,
fighting battles, waging wars,
swearing I don't hold a grudge,
while keeping scores.

Weary from the weight of worry,
burdened by my daily chores,
frightened that the next blow
lands me on all fours.

Trying hard to do things my way,
seeking still to guide the oars,
thinking *I'm* the one who
opens all the doors.

Searching for the power within,
grasping toward the dream that soars
out of reach, until Your presence
through me pours.

I lose nothing of myself
by saying, "Not my will, but Yours."
Grant, oh Lord, the peace
to quiet my spirit's roars.

PATTERNS AND MYTHS

She's taking on another name,
"This time," she says, "it's right."
The others didn't fit, so now
she's racing through the night to catch the day.
"This time," she says, "the magic's here to stay."

She says she's very sure this time,
of what she wants to do,
but she checked with all her brothers first,
as if they had a clue to what she needs.
Why is it only male advice she heeds?

She thinks it's not the same mistake
if it's with a different lover.
The pattern still eludes her,
and the fairy tales still hover in her mind,
as she seeks the answer in the ties that bind.

She's searching for the perfect man,
to realize her dreams,
someone who'll be all things to her
and quiet the muffled screams, the nameless fear
of gazing sadly in an empty mirror.

STORMS

The storm came up quite suddenly
that gentle summer day.
I feared the wind and lightning
would carry me away.

I sought the safety of Daddy's lap
to hold my fears at bay,
and he told that frightened little girl,
"The storm will pass away."

I'm not sure I believed him then,
the sky was dark and gray,
and it seemed the rain and thunder
had likely come to stay.

But safe there on the sheltered porch
I heard my father say,
"The rain is music to the earth.
The storm will pass away."

I tried to hear the things he heard,
watched hard ground turn to clay
to feed the flowers and make them grow
when the storm had passed away.

The fireworks in the heavens
formed an awe-inspiring display,
and I ceased to be so anxious
for the storm to pass away.

As the thunder descrescendoed
and the rain became fine spray,
I found an abiding love of storms
with me to this day.

Several decades later,
in an equally magnificent array
of power and of beauty,
my father passed away.

It seemed a fitting exit
and I know what he would say:
"The grief you feel, just like the storm,
will also pass away."

The truth within my father's words
brings both comfort and dismay,
for whether blinding pain or brilliant joy,
the storm will pass away.

GRACE

Above our chaos,
Order.
Beneath our turmoil,
Peace.

Despite our prejudice,
Acceptance.
Beyond our sorrow,
Joy.

Preceding our transgressions,
Forgiveness.
Beside our stinginess,
Benevolence.

After our blindness,
Sight.
Before our need,
Love.

FOR MAMA

This is a poem to my mother, Iris,
with whom I am inextricably bound
in countless ways, including
"You must be Iris's girl,"
though I never really saw it.
How much else have I not seen,
thinking – as I must have –
that *your* life began with *me*?
What young dreams did you give up
for love,
or duty,
or lack of opportunity?
What grace enabled you
to give so much
and ask so little?
I want you to know
that through your faith and steadfastness,
your genuine delight and ready forgiveness,
your never being too busy to play
    "You know what? I love you!"
you have given me
not just the gift of love,
but a greater, rarer gift:
the capacity to believe I'm worthy to *be* loved.

Knowing that what we are
shows in our faces,
I am surprised and pleased these days,
when I glance in a store window as I pass
and for just a moment, see you.
So I write this for you, Mama,
for the threads that connect us,
because

  you know what?

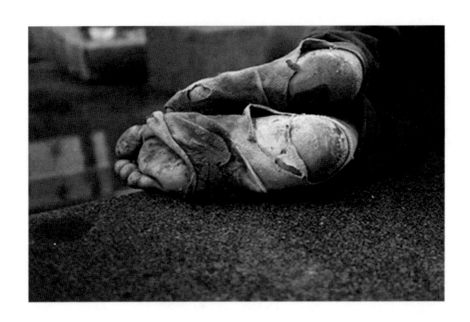

THE LEAST OF THESE

A homeless man sits on a corner near
a store I frequent for my daily needs
of candy or of cokes – essential things
to fuel the frantic pace I set myself.

He only sits, he neither begs nor pleads,
approaches no one, asks for no handouts,
but occupies himself in calm repose
amid the odd assortment of his life.
No means has he for moving place to place,
no cart appropriated from The Max
or Carnival. Instead his worldly goods
are wrapped, like him, in shades of Army green
and gray, and stacked around, concealed in rolls
which form a barricade and cushion on
the concrete homestead where he stakes his claim.

Sometimes he disappears, I wonder where.
I'd like to think a shelter, rows of beds
and soup to warm and nourish, or to a friend
who, when the elements are most severe,
will take him in and give him respite from
the harshest days and nights our clime bestows.
But seeing him emerge from buildings long
abandoned, or from dumpsters, makes me think
more likely he has nowhere else to go.

What circumstance has brought him to this fate?
Did he get down-sized, cut back, laid off, fired?

He seems alert, but still uncomprehending,
his mind erased by drugs and alcohol,
or elevated to some higher plane
of wisdom and serenity profound,
accepting all that falls to him with heart
and mind and soul somehow at peace within.

And on those Sundays he comes to my church,
is it for worship, or for warmth and food?
And do I hold him just a bit at bay,
with nostrils flared and eyebrows raised in scorn?

Pray let him find the outstretched hand of love,
the open heart which knows the deeper truth:
that there, but for the grace of God, go I.

HUNGER

You make me hungry.

Your heat sends me straight to the kitchen
in a frenzy for other cravings:
    thick sliced bacon,
    peppered crisp and salty,
        juices flowing in remembrance
        of the brine of your exertion;
    buttery English muffins,
    warm and toasted,
        honey dripping like love,
        coating fingers whose only primal knowledge
        is reading the codes and contours of your body;
    orange rind and black pekoe
    rising on steam,
        a startling reminder
        that there is any scent in the world
        save yours.

You make me hungry.

Your need pulls me back
for appetites yet unappeased.
I turn my face back and forth,
back and forth
through the hair on your chest.
Feline-like, I inhale you
open-mouthed.

"Yes, yes," you whisper
and your voice surrounds me,
reverberates in my ears,
hums in my throat.

I watch you watching me
until sunspots flicker at the edge of my vision,
blinding me to all but the entwinement of
    arms, tongues, fingers, toes.
I want to wrap gossamer legs around you,
encase you,
absorb you,
breathe your breath,
carry you with me into fevered flight
until we soar in tandem above the current,
until *my* satisfaction
sates *your* hunger, too.

You make me hungry.

A MATTER OF TRUST

Our love took root in common ground of pain,
but first you watched with subtle smile, and sly.
You saw each shadow pass across my eye,
yet never turned away or judged the stain
of wounds and wrongs that live in love's domain.
And in the scars, which neither could deny,
the gift of faith was found, a borning cry
where mirrored peace and passion held free reign.
Two prodigals, returned to self at last,
acceptance of our truest souls, the prize.
I laid aside the armor and the shield.
I *chose* to disbelieve the die was cast,
as now I weigh truth against disguise,
and bind the lacerations there revealed.

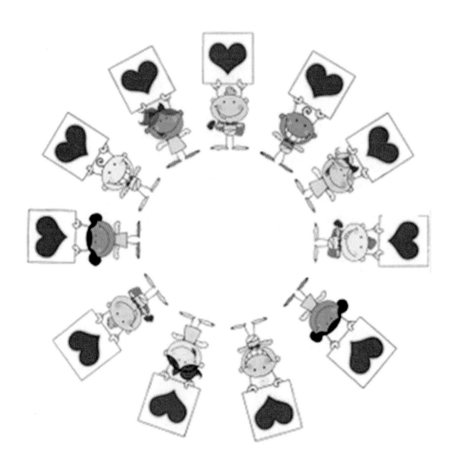

STRENGTH FOR THE JOURNEY

Hearts of sadness,
Hearts of weeping,
Hearts of sorrow overflowing,
From the wellspring of compassion,
Through the fire of fear and longing,
By sisterhood's silken sinews,
Hearts of love still growing.

Hearts of glee and
Hearts of gladness,
Hearts of raucous laughter ringing,
From the core of common virtue,
Through the hail of hurt and anguish,
By the melody of the mavens,
Hearts of joy still singing.

Hearts of fortitude,
Hearts of passion,
Hearts of deepest substance mining,
From the nurturing of vision,
Through the dying dreams and darkness,
By the power of hands united,
Hearts of light still shining.

CHOICES

Movement comes in fits and starts,
accomplishments measured in pieces and parts,
and I may never touch the hearts
of anyone who doesn't already love me.
For I have watched from the other shore,
the rite of passage through that door,
requiring all, and maybe more,
yes, even more.

It isn't possible to gauge
what's won or lost by a given age,
though a choice between doors within a cage
has nothing at all to do with being free.
But the dreams that filter through the years
of silences and surging fears,
are purified by fiery tears,
by gentle tears.

ISCARIOT

That's right, that's right, I am the one.
And who are you to judge? You only sweep
the courts for them, and when you're done,
you hurry off to home and hearth and sleep.
I tried to give it back, you know.
I didn't want their money, not like that!
God knows we need the money, though,
but high and mighty, they refused. They spat
on me and laughed and turned away,
as if they hadn't heard a word I'd said.
With blood-stained coins they got their way,
a spiteful trick, and now it's on *my* head.
I loved him better than the rest,
not blind to all our needs and what things cost.
I thought I'd put him to the test
and he'd be forced to stand. Now all is lost.
The crowds are screaming "Crucify!"
And in your eyes I see the curse of blame.
I loved him best, but only I
will bear the cruelest double cross of shame.

NEW YORK

It's several years since I saw you
twenty-five since I lived there
and yet – like Barbra and Billy
I am forever
in a "New York State of Mind"
big apple
"bright lights, big city"
as much a part of me as Cowtown
or Burleson
living in the East Village
living in Chelsea
living in East Harlem
working in mid-town
working on the upper west side
working in Soho
the best food in the world
the freshest produce
2nd Avenue Deli (better than the Carnegie)
Café Reggio
The Royal Indian
Balducci's
bagels (*real* bagels)
chestnuts roasting on an open…
street vendor's cart
music everywhere
jazz in the air

The Vanguard
The Blue Note
Sweet Basil
Seventh Avenue South
Chet Baker
Walter Booker
Woody Shaw
Cecil McBee
Randy Brecker
Michael Brecker
John Scofield
Art Blakey
Branford Marsalis
Wynton Marsalis
Jimmy Cobb
Bobbie McFerrin
Dan Fogelberg
James Taylor
Joni Mitchell
Herbie Hancock
Dizzy Gillespie
Miles Davis
MILES DAVIS
MILES DAVIS!!!
street musicians on every corner
from Columbus Circle
to Times Square
to Washington Square Park
to the World Trade Towers

and on every cross street in between
and in every subway station known to man
Broadway
and off-Broadway
and off-off-Broadway
the Empire
the top of the Empire
the top of the Empire at night
starry, starry night
I mean the original
the Van Gogh
up close and personal
the actual canvas on which his genius took shape
rooms full of his canvases
more than the heart can hold
and writing
and more writing
and more writing still
and parks
and trees
and a profusion of daffodils
in the middle of rush hour
and life
and hope
and possibility
always possibility
it is *never* too late
in New York!

TRANSFORMATION

The unrelenting wind bends the trees,

bows them,

angles them amid the forest's vertical order.

Inexorable howling

transforming the landscape,

softening its rigidity.

So, too, sorrow shape-shifts into sensitivity,

conflict into compassion,

shame into understanding,

deprivation into generosity,

injury into forgiveness,

pain into tenderness,

bent by the breath of inexhaustible,

unrelenting

Love.

QUESTIONS ON ENTERING MY 40TH YEAR
(Perceptions of Non-conception)

What lunar pull,
matched,
stretched taut by what anchor,
assures certain knowledge
of the sweetness for which my emptiness longs?
How can I know what I've never known?
How can emptiness rise from a well?
What kind of bargain is it,
where even the bending of my will cannot fill the void?
At what point acceptance?
At what price?
Is it not enough
to see how casually that which I long for is accomplished
by those who have no longing?
Must I also deny the loss?
Is it not enough
to recognize other gains?
Must I also repress the grief?
Is it not enough
to appreciate the irony of pointless precaution?
Must I also be gracious to those,
who from their privileged status,
declare I'm better off?
Am I?

Is it selfishness

that insists on a specific expression of oneness?

Is it conceit

that suggests there is much to offer?

Is it indulgence

That yearns to know the circle completed?

Is it arrogance

that exclaims, "Surely it cannot stop with me!"?

Is infinity merely the richest fantasy?

How else to explain

why a soul so blessed

still cries into the night

Unfair,

Unfair.

FULFILLMENT

The path to peace has always been surrender.
No matter the scale: cocoon or cross –
Surrender.
From daybreak in Eden
to the rainbow on Ararat –
Surrender.
On the altar at Moriah
or in the flame on Horeb –
Surrender.
The yielding that relinquishes,
leaves behind,
resigns the will,
implores mercy –
Surrender.
The innocent in Nazareth
unhesitating, "Let it be to me…" –
Surrender.
The birth in Bethlehem,
comprehending Calvary –
Surrender.
And in its harvest,
inexplicable joy,
hope,
peace.

ABOUT THE AUTHOR

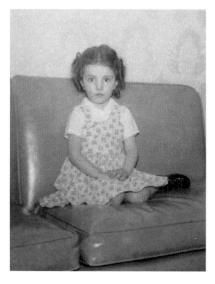

Mary-margaret Belota began life as Mary Margaret Burns. She is a born and raised Texan who sojourned for a time in New York City and feels equally at home in both places.

She graduated from Texas Wesleyan College (now University) in Fort Worth, Texas, and worked for many years in corporate America. In 2001, she made the best career move of her life and became a teacher, first in the regular classroom, and then as a music teacher for all elementary grades. She now rejoices in her retirement!

She has been singing, performing, and writing since childhood, though her penchant for theater was not realized as a performer until much later. She has been published in several small journals, and in 2012 she won the Val Wilkie Educator Award in writing to attend the Mayborn School of Journalism's annual Literary Non-fiction Conference.

This is Ms. Belota's first volume of poetry. She is currently compiling two other volumes including one of Christmas poems.

And... she is not nearly as well behaved as the above picture might suggest.

Made in the USA
Columbia, SC
24 June 2023